T0198846

Finding Momma's
Notebook

This is a true story about finding a notebook that held memories of my parents love, faith, illness, pain, and heartbreak, and of the faith that guided them through it all.

CINDY NELSON SMITH

WESTBOW
PRESS
A DIVISION OF THOMAS NELSON

WestBow Press books may be ordered through booksellers or by contacting:

WestBow Press
A Division of Thomas Nelson
1663 Liberty Drive
Bloomington, IN 47403
www.westbowpress.com
1-(866) 928-1240

ISBN: 978-1-4497-2883-0 (sc)
ISBN: 978-1-4497-2882-3 (e)

Library of Congress Control Number: 2011918270

Printed in the United States of America

WestBow Press rev. date: 10/22/2011

I dedicate this book
to my family to ensure
that they will always
know the legacy of the
faith within my parents.

Acknowledgements

God for blessing me with such wonderful spirit-filled
parents and for His awesome presence, wonderful love,
beautiful peace, faithful strength, forgiveness and a grace
that truly is sufficient; and for giving us His Word, the Bible,
which is full of amazing scriptures and promises
for every event that happens in life;
Momma for writing a notebook that held her inner-most
thoughts; which inspired me to write this book; my family:
my husband, daughters, son-in-law, sister, brother, sister in
law, daughter-in-law and step son, grandchildren, nieces,
nephews, a special aunt, aunts, cousins, and friends.
Pastor and his wife, who are also my friends; all of the
preachers that prayed and visited Momma and Daddy; the
ladies that brought all of the meals to our family; the heart
transplant team: doctors, surgeons, and nurses;
the Oncology team: doctors and nurses;
"Tiger girl," from Home Health and Hospice; our family
doctor in Mississippi; the folks at the funeral home who
helped so much; and everyone who prayed for us,
gave hugs, and held us up in our time
of need.

I want to thank my daughter
Jessica Smith Taylor
For editing
This book
For me

Preface

This book is for anyone who may go through trials in life that seem too heavy to bear. We need to trust that we have a Heavenly Father who created us and loved us so much that He would send his Son to die for the sins that separated us from Him. He sent a Comforter just like Jesus promised. That Holy Spirit is the very presence that walks with us daily. Sometimes He carries us and we don't even know it, until we look back and say how did I make it through that? That's when we praise God with a thankful heart, knowing He is with us and He will never leave us or forsake us. He didn't create us to walk on this earth without Him. He created all of us to love and guide us; if we have faith and know that faith is: "The substance of things hoped for, the evidence of things not seen. (Hebrews 11:1)

Table of Contents

Chapter 1

Finding the Notebook

Hebrews 4:16
KJV

"Let us therefore
come boldly unto
the throne of grace,
that we may obtain mercy,
and find grace to
help in time of need."

I walked up the steps to the porch. The two wooden rocking chairs sitting there, one had a green cushion for the back and seat. She had made them for him so that he would be more comfortable as he would sit outside to get some fresh air. The humming bird feeder was empty. Empty hanging flower pots hung from the chains on the porch. It wasn't time to replant flowers yet. Wind chimes making a sweet sound in the cool breeze, with the word *Welcome* on the top, hung from the rafters. As I looked at the door there was the ramp that we worked so hard to get right, just for him so that he would not miss the step into the door. I opened the screen door and knocked. My sister opened it. This would be her home now, but first we had things to do. I hugged her neck and we began to cry. This would not be an easy task, but things had to be done.

The walls were decorated with her beautiful oil paintings. She had worked so hard on the Magnolia that was on the big canvas, along with other paintings of granddaddy's barn, lighthouses, landscapes with mountains, waterfalls, and tranquil life vases with Calla Lilies gently placed in them. She loved to paint; she was a natural. Her signature was at the bottom of each canvas. The shadow boxes of the arrow heads that he had collected over the years hung along the walls, down the hall. Each arrow head placed on white cotton in different arrangements. He had searched for the perfect ones on his adventures of arrow head hunting in the woods. She had worked hard placing each one to display his findings. Some of the shadow boxes were large and some were small.

Looking to the other side of the room were two blue recliners. On the back of one was the dark blue Ole Miss Insignia blanket. A red pillow placed in the seat of the chair. Beside the recliner was a TV tray and on it sat his breathing treatment machine. On the back of the other recliner was a tan and white Afghan that she had made. Between the chairs was an end table that they had for as long as I can remember. Along the other wall was the old wooden couch with cushions that she would re-upholster every few years to match the new curtains that she would sew.

A tall book case was standing against the wall. The shelves were full of a variety of books. His books were on the two bottom shelves, books about the Civil War, Indians, and arrow heads. He looked up every arrow head he found wanting to know what each piece was created for. Among his books, the most important one was his giant print Bible and some old Sunday school books. The upper shelves held her books. She loved to read and study about God, Jesus and The Holy Spirit. I picked up one of the books, her handwritten notes in the margins of so many pages. Underlining certain sentences and some highlighted because the words meant something special to her. Across the room was another shelf, again full of books, some hard back and some paper back. Most were about God's love. Some of the books were about flowers, perennials, annuals, and wildflowers, both indoor and outdoor. On the shelves were also some angel figurines, a figure of the "The Lord's Supper," and her favorite, the statute of Jesus praying in the garden of Gethsemane.

The big buffet cabinet was against another wall. It once belonged to her mother. Opening the top drawer, I knew what was in there, the pill planners for him. There were four that held his medicine for seven days. Most of them were completely full, we had just filled them. There were so many pills, not only in the planners but also in the bottles. There was the purple binder that held the list of each medication name, dosage, and prescribed daily amount when it had to be renewed and ordered, along with his medical history that I had made for him. I closed the drawer.

I walked down the hallway where the shadow boxes hung toward the middle bedroom. It wasn't really a bedroom it was *her* room. There was the tan cabinet that held the Singer Sewing Machine that she had for as long as I could remember. The little bulletin board on the wall over the sewing machine that had each one of the family's clothing measurements. Each grandchild and great-grandchild's name was there and some were marked through and changed as the kids would grow out of a size. Beside the cabinet were clear boxes of material, with every color and design you could imagine and every color thread that she needed. On the other side of the room were her canvases. She had started drawing out the picture she was going to paint. Her paint brushes in a container and all of the oil colors were in another clear cabinet with drawers. Opening the closet were blank white canvases that she had intended on painting.

The kitchen had some dishes in the sink from his last meal. The yellow and white checked curtains she had made hung over the sink. In the window was a white lace angel with the words "Be still and know that I am God." Psalm 46:10. (KJV) By the window was her blue bird of happiness that was given to her by my daughter. On the refrigerator were taped pictures of the family and get well cards. On the door to the utility room was a large calendar with days marked with the doctor's appointments that each of them had. Also on the calendar was every family member's birthdays. Taped to the wall beside the calendar were business cards of all of the doctors they had seen and still needed to see. There had to be some type of organization to the chaos. On the cabinets of the kitchen was of course the coffee pot, they had to have their coffee in the morning. Her convection oven that she would bake cookies and cakes in was sitting there. On the center cabinet of the kitchen were the flowers that we had given her for her birthday, Day Lilies and Irises that were now drooping and almost falling off the stems.

After walking through the kitchen, I went into their bedroom with the furniture that they had for so many years. Family photos hung on the walls, they could lie in the bed and look at us any time they wanted to. Family was important to them. Beside the bed was a nightstand that had her Bible on it. In his closet, the first thing I saw was his suspenders of several different colors. I reached to smell one of his Sunday dress shirts; it smelled of Old Spice cologne, just like him. Looking more I saw his T-shirts that read on the front "Worlds' Best Papa," "#1 Dad," and of course the worn out Ole Miss T-shirts. In the bottom of the closet were his shoes. She had bought him so many sandals trying to fit his swollen feet. In the back of the closet was his old shoe shine box. He had that box forever; his shoes had to shine and be clean for church. He had to look his best, and he always did.

Her closet was full of dresses and turtle neck shirts to cover up the scars of surgery. Two T-shirts I reached for and they read on the front, "Mother and Daughter by Chance-Friends by Choice," and "A Grandmother's Love means sew much'." Her beautiful dresses that she had sewed were hanging there. On the back of the door hung a shoe rack that held all of her shoes for her very small feet.

In the bathroom, hanging on a rack were their housecoats and a shelf holding his pajamas. By the sink was his razor and after shave lotion. Opening the bottle I could smell him. On the walls of the bathroom were silver handles that would help him move around easier and mostly to help him not fall. Although, at 1o'clock one morning it didn't work and I looked at the floor remembering and thought to myself, "how awful it was that he had to crawl to the bed and we had to lift and pull him to help him get back in bed."

On the other side of the bedroom was a file cabinet. We knew we had to go through it. We sat on the floor and opened the top drawer. We began to go through each file getting out the papers that we needed and leaving the ones we didn't. In there was a lot of history, their marriage license from 58 years ago, birth certificates, his pharmacy license and Navy papers, and so much more. We continued looking. Toward the back of the second drawer was a maroon notebook. I pulled it out. As I sat on the floor in front of the cabinet I opened the book. It was her handwriting on every page, some were written in blue ink and some black. At the top of the first page was the year 1998. I flipped through the pages seeing dates and times written down. Her thoughts, feelings and emotions for ten years were there in black and blue ink on the pages of the notebook. I told my sister, *"I can't read this now. Not now, not today."* I put it to the side.

Chapter 2

Reading the Notebook

Daniel 10: 18-19
KJV

"Then there came again and touched me
one like the appearance of a man, and he
strengthen me.
And said, Oh man greatly loved,
Fear not: peace be unto thee, be strong,
yea, be strong.
And when he had spoken unto me, I was
strengthened, and said Let my lord speak
for thou hast
strengthened me."

A year later I began cleaning an upstairs bedroom. It had become a room that everything gets put in, you know one of those rooms you put stuff in that you will get to later, well it was now later. It was also the room that I had put a lot of Momma and Daddy's belongings in. In the corner was a table that I had put some of their things on. It was their important papers and things I had that I wanted to keep. I knew it was time to put all of it away in a special place. *"I can do it now,"* I thought to myself. The plastic funeral packages for both of my parents were laying there with the obituaries, sign in books, and notes of who sent flowers were on the table, zipped closed. I placed them in a box. All of the pictures we had used at the funeral home were placed in the box as well. The file folders that I had taken from the file cabinet were on the table, these also went in the box. Under the folders there it was . . . the maroon notebook. I thought *what is this?* Then it hit me, I remembered sitting on the floor of their home a year before looking through that file cabinet and putting the notebook off to the side. I took a very deep breath and opened the book.

I sat there "indian style" on the floor, put the notebook in my lap and began to read. I read Momma's words that she had written over four years from when all of the illness started for her and Daddy. As I read the dates, times, and the events of their life I began remembering life with my family. I knew what they had been through, our family knew what had happened over those years, but these words came from Momma's heart. I read every word, some through tears of remembering the anxiety, frustrations, pain, hurt, and disappointments. Momma's prayers to God were written down, her conversations that she had with Him. It was though her handwriting would start slow in a sentence and then when she got an answer to a prayer she could not write fast enough. It was all there. What a gift she had left for me, for all of us.

In the notebook were pages of dates and times of the first four years when she was diagnosed with the first cancer and Daddy was diagnosed with multiple silent heart attacks, which all began in 1998. As I turned each page I could recall all the doctor's names. Each entry was defined by an illness and what happened at the appointment. Most appointments with one doctor would lead to seeing another one for some complication or further testing of the diagnosis. It was a way for Momma to keep up with everything, but also for her to write down her emotions. As I read I could see that she used this as an outlet for her emotions. She would write when she or Daddy would have a good day or when the day was bad, or days of physical exhaustion due to treatments or changing medications or days of *"we are feeling good and having a great day."* Times of when each was in the hospital, and for what reason and even how long they were there. Reading Momma's writing on each page brought back memories of a lot of tough times, but then she would put words of how her faith was weak and then she would gain strength.

Now as I am holding the notebook in my lap, I see the words and feel her emotions. I begin to understand. Most of all I understand that she had left this for me to share. When people we love so dearly go through tough times and take the time to write it all down there must be a reason. I saw it as a release for her from her heart, to the pen, to the paper in the notebook. As I look at each word, I could hear her voice reading them to me and I could see and remember all the events as they happened. I was reliving everything but this time it was different. They were in Heaven and I was here reading this all alone, I was crying and Momma and Daddy were not here to hold me. Daddy could not give me his words of wisdom. I was on my own, how lonely to not have my parents with me anymore. *"Oh my Lord!"* I cried.

Then I began to pray, "Father please help me, I've tried to be so strong, I have understood the questions of the situation through most of it. Your Word says, "You will not forsake me," and I really need Your strong arms holding me now. As I continued to read I could feel God strengthen me through her words and I began to receive strength to continue reading. This is the strength that God gave me to write this book. I knew what I had to do.

Momma's notebook was about trials, her and Daddy's illness, and the faith that brought them through it.

Chapter 3

They Shall Become One Flesh

Genesis 2:24
KJV

"Therefore shall a man shall leave
his father and his mother
and cleave unto his wife,
and they shall
be one flesh."

Before I can tell you about what happened in the years after 1998, I must start with the beginning. Both of my parents were born in 1934. Daddy was born in July and Momma in January. They always laughed and said that since Momma was 6 months older, she could be the boss from January until July. After Daddy's birthday in July then he could be the boss the rest of the year. Although, we all knew that Momma was the boss all year round.

Daddy played football, basketball, and baseball. Momma was a cheerleader. They were high school sweethearts. Both graduated the class of 1952 from a small high school in a beautiful country town in Mississippi.

They were married by the Justice of the Peace on November 17, 1952. I can see them standing there hand in hand saying wedding vows, *"I take you through sickness and in health until death do us part."* The words rolled off the tongues so easily because it was true. They were always so in love.

Most newlyweds plan a special place to go on the honeymoon. Daddy planned theirs driving up the road about 10 miles to a basketball game. Momma didn't complain she was with her husband and she didn't care as long as they were together.

A few years later, Daddy joined the Navy. He was stationed in Guam. He got Momma there and that is where my oldest brother was born. When Momma went into labor, Daddy and his Navy Buddy dropped Momma off at the hospital and went to basketball game. When they got back to the hospital, Momma said, "Come and meet your son." For some reason Momma understood this was just the way it was. She didn't seem to mind. They would always laugh when the story was told.

After Daddy got out of the Navy, they moved backed to Mississippi where Daddy put himself through Pharmacy school at Ole Miss. While Daddy was in college, Momma gave birth to another son, a daughter, and then I was born the year that Daddy graduated from College. A career and a family, life is good. Then we moved back to the town where it all began.

Daddy worked as a Pharmacist with a very sweet man until the man retired. He sold Daddy the drug store. Momma worked with him doing the business part of the store. All four of us kids worked there working the cash register, vacuuming, making deliveries, and whatever we were asked to do. Daddy worked a lot of hours in that store and was always on call if someone needed a prescription filled.

Our family life was what I would call normal. We had our summer vacations. We played flag football in the yard and basketball where Daddy would call a foul on everybody but himself. Usually the teams were Momma and the boys against Daddy and us girls, my sister and me. They loved playing tennis. Daddy had the best left handed forehand. He could put a spin on that ball that could run anyone all over the court. He loved to watch us work to hit it back to him.

Momma and Daddy had their share of problems throughout their marriage. They had, like all married couples, hard times, trials, temptations, and arguments.

Also as individuals that had their own inward battles that they had to deal with, face, and overcome. Through it all their love became stronger and laid a concrete foundation that helped them through the last ten years of their lives.

Chapter 4

Momma

Ephesians 3:17-19
KJV

"That Christ may dwell in your hearts
by faith:
being rooted
and grounded
in love, may be able to
comprehend with all the
saints what
is the breadth and length
and depth, and height;
And to know the Love of Christ
which passeth knowledge;
that ye might be filled
with all the fullness of God."

Now let me tell you about my Momma first, since she was the oldest. One of my brothers said it the best, "When we were young she was like a chainsaw, feisty and tough, but as she got older she calmed down to a weed eater, a little less feisty and less tough." Momma could have invented sticky notes; she would write notes on a piece of paper and the notes would be everywhere. She taped them over the commode that said *lift the toilet seat,* (this one was for the boys and Daddy), or on the bathroom mirror, *clean up your mess.*

I will never forget how often she would correct anyone's grammar. "Ain't is not a word," she would always say.

I guess she loved to cook or maybe it was just because Daddy loved to eat. She was always in the kitchen. She, as much as I can remember, would fix Daddy's plate and bring it to him. Always making a dessert, Daddy loved sweets, especially cookies and fudge.

She was from Mississippi but born in California because her Daddy was a Navy man. I'm not sure when Momma, her little sister, and parents moved back home.

Her Daddy was a tall man we called him Big Daddy, and her Mom was tiny, I don't think she was even 5 feet tall. I don't know why we called her Big Momma or Biggie because she was so tiny. Momma's dad died when I was young so I don't really remember him. Biggie lived with us when we were young and when my parents built our house in the country on his parent's land, where he grew up as a child, they built an apartment connected to it and that is where Biggie lived for a long time. I recall how much Momma loved her Grandmother; she talked about her a lot.

Momma had her chair by Daddy's, it was surrounded by books. She could not read enough about The Father, Son, and The Holy Spirit. She would study for hours, underlining words that would touch her and write things down to remember. Her hand written notes on every page saying, "*this is important* or *I love this.*" She loved books about prayer, how to live a Christian life, Heaven, and God's mercy and grace.

When she wasn't reading or cooking, she was sewing. She made a lot of our clothes, beautiful curtains for the house, and she learned to upholster furniture. She loved that old sewing machine. Momma made all of mine and my sister's baton and cheerleader uniforms and some of the other girl's on the team as well. She made Daddy's pajamas, and all of us had a pair of pajama pants that she had made for Christmas one year. She would make beauty pageant dressing for the grandchildren and she even made some of the granddaughter's wedding dresses. She enjoyed seeing the family smile with her gifts. She wanted to pass on her sewing and taught my sister and me to sew. She also taught her oldest two granddaughters. She always said when I die; bury my sewing machine with me.

She knitted Afghans, big and small and all different colors. She also would make crafts with her hands. Her mind never stopped about what she could make.

Then she fell in love with oil painting. She was a natural. She started with Magnolias, which were her favorite, then barns, mountain scenes, and still life. Momma would come out of her painting room with paint usually somewhere on her face, her hands, and clothes. She didn't care; she was having fun and enjoyed every minute of it!

If you could not find Momma she was usually in the yard. She would say that her flowerbeds were her church. I think she had about 20 different colors of Daylilies, which was her and Daddy's favorite. Daddy would fuss every time that she would go and buy more flowers for the yard, but he loved them too. She would spend hours planting and talking to God. She would tell God how beautiful He made the flowers. It was there she would pour her heart out to the Lord. She would come out of the yard with dirt all on her hands and usually on her backside where she would wipe her hands. Most of all, whatever burden she had been carrying was left out there in that dirt somewhere because that is where she left it with God.

Momma would say that her Holy Spirit was on her left shoulder, and she would pat her shoulder and smile.

She loved Daddy so much and loved her children, grandchildren, and great-grandchildren. When my oldest daughter was beginning labor with her second child, Momma came to Louisiana from Mississippi and told my daughter, "Okay

I'm here now, you can have the baby," and she did. This was on Momma's birthday and that meant so much to her.

She took turns with the other ladies at church teaching Sunday school. It was called Hope Sunday School class. She gave the classroom a picture that she had painted of praying hands. She really loved the ladies in the class. They all got together and made banners for the church for special occasions.

Momma was tough. She tried to keep us all in line. She was not one to hold her tongue. Everyone knew her thoughts because she did not hesitate to tell you like it was.

Momma was tiny like her Mom, about 5 feet 2. She is a beautiful woman with beautiful medium brown hair and big green eyes. If we were in trouble her green eyes would get even bigger and we knew we were in trouble.

Chapter 5

Daddy

Mark 12:30
KJV

"And thou shalt love the Lord thy God
with all thy heart,
with all thy soul,
with all thy mind,
and with all thy strength:
this is the first commandment."

Anyone that would take his new bride to a basketball game on their honeymoon must really love sports. Yep, that's Daddy. It really didn't matter the sport as long as there was a ball involved, he was there. He coached my brothers from peewee league to pony league in baseball. He would watch a College football game or basketball game on TV and beside him would be a radio, and he would be listening to a different ball game. I don't know how he kept up with both, but he did.

Daddy loved to work, he loved being a pharmacist. He would stand behind that counter and count out pills for hours. But he always made time to pull a silly prank on someone in the store. Daddy worked hard. He genuinely cared for every person that came in the drug store. He handled each medication as if he was filling it for a family member. He took time to talk to people about their medicine.

At home you never knew what may be in your shoes when you went to put then on, a rock or paper, just something for him to leave his mark that he had done something. No matter how busy he was he always smiled, with a smile that would light up a room. Sometimes he made silly smiles that would make you laugh and it would always make someone feel better.

Daddy was the one who would hang lizards on his ears and try to put them on anyone that would let him. All the grandchildren would know if Papa's got a lizard you better run. He also loved to pull toes; if you were relaxed with your feet propped up he would pull your toes until they popped. The more you told him "Stop," the more he would try.

All of the grandchildren were girls. Daddy would say at least he would have enough for a basketball team. When the first great grandchild came along, it was a boy. He was even born on Daddy's birthday. He was very proud. He never had favorites even among us children. He loved each one of us unconditionally.

Daddy loved to sing. He would sing, *"You are my sunshine"* and *"I love you a bushel and a peck."* He would mostly sing the songs silly and dance a jig. In church he would sing softly but with strength to his God. However, when we sang *"How Great Thou Art,"* he would get that beautiful voice a little louder.

When any of us girls (daughters, granddaughters or great-granddaughters) would walk in the room where Daddy was, he would always say, "Hey Boy!" We never understood why we were all called boys. Of course, the girls would say, "I'm not a boy, Papa." He would make a silly face and usually throw something at you. Sometimes I think he really meant for us girls to be boys because he would not hesitate to wrestle with us and I mean on the floor wrestling, real wrestling. When it got too rough, Momma would holler and tell us to stop. Usually we would keep going and she would end up on the floor with us.

Daddy would always call us on the phone and say, "I just wanted to call and see what you looked like" or "I just wanted to hear your sweet little voice."

Now, by Daddy's chair were newspapers, normally with the sports section open, junk food, and a radio. He also had his hiding places where if he knew someone, like my husband, was coming over he would hide his special fudge and leave just enough to say he shared.

Daddy has collected old coins as long as I can remember. He kept the coins in little jars and an old money bag. He would usually give the grandchildren and then the great grandchildren a coin on their birthdays. He had a lot of 50 cent pieces and silver dollars.

After retiring, Daddy became very interested in exploring and looking for arrowheads. Anywhere trees had recently been cut down and the ground had been tilled up, he was there. He would read about the different pieces he found. He would sit and show all the children what he found and explain how the Indians used that certain piece.

Daddy loved God. He was the only son of faithful, Christian parents. He had an older sister and a younger sister. He was raised on a farm. His Daddy was a deacon at the church. He was a farmer and he worked for the Highway Department. His mother loved to sew. I remember aprons and bonnets that she had made. She was also very involved in church.

He loved to talk about how it was when he was young. He was proud that his family was the first in the community to get indoor plumbing. He never had a brother so he was very close to his uncles that were close to his age.

He became a deacon in the Church in 1984. This was not something that he took for granted. It was a blessing from God. He knew it. Daddy's faith was in his actions and how he lived life. He read his bible and studied his Sunday school lesson every week.

If we got out of line, he was not the one to spank us, he would talk to us. Sometimes I think we all would have rather got the spanking. His words were strong and made us who we are today. Daddy led by example. He did what Jesus told us to do, love and serve.

Daddy was about 5 foot 8. He had small blue eyes. Like his mom, he had black hair, very thick and wavy. The grandchildren saw his high school pictures and would say how handsome Papa is. Daddy loved that.

Chapter 6

Daddy's Heart Attacks and Momma's Cancer

Isaiah 43:2-3a
KJV

"When thou passeth through the waters,
I will be with thee:
And through the rivers,
They shall not overflow thee:
When thou walkest through the fire,
thou shalt not be burned,
neither shall the flame kindle upon thee.
For I am the Lord thy God."

Now that you know a little bit about the beginning, I will tell more about where the notebook began. Daddy got sick first. He found out in the early 1990's that he had had several silent heart attacks. He was going to open the drug store one morning and passed out. He began to start taking medication and seemed to be doing well.

In November of 1998, Daddy was walking and was found by our neighbor in the road, she called the ambulance and he was taken to the hospital there in Mississippi and then by helicopter taken to a hospital in Baton Rouge. We were told that he had had more heart attacks. Daddy never had chest pain, but there was a lot of damage to his heart. He was very sick. It was so hard for Daddy. It was hard for all of us to watch our strong Daddy lay in that hospital bed day after day. Daddy was on a ventilator for a short time and was finally weaned off of that. We all were relieved and thanked God that he would be well again.

While Daddy was in the hospital, Momma and I were sitting in the waiting room. She looked at me and said, "Feel this knot on the side of my neck." I felt a large knot on the left side of her neck. We knew it needed to be seen about, but she felt that she had to wait for Daddy to get better.

Well, when Daddy got out of the hospital Momma went to check on the "knot". This was 13 days after Daddy came home. She went to a specialist and found out that it was the big C-word . . . Momma had cancer. They both needed healing. They both turned to the God that they loved and trusted. When Momma first learned that she had cancer, in the notebook, she wrote

"How do we respond when adversity comes into our lives? When I first learned I had cancer-I was so brave—I had so much faith and trust in God—I was convinced that this cancer was part of a plan God had for my life. This is so simple to say and to believe until reality sets in and we are actually put to the test. I read there are three great truths to be learned through adversity. 1. We can never see the beginning from the ending of God's plan for our lives because God sees the big picture. 2. All adversities in our lives must first be sifted

through the permissive will of God. 3. God will not test us beyond our ability to endure."

On December 7, 1998, my aunt took Momma to Jackson, Mississippi for her chemotherapy, while on the same day my sister and I had Daddy in New Orleans, Louisiana for an evaluation of a heart transplant. The transplant team told us that Daddy would be put on the transplant list, but because he was able to live at home, it would take a while. Daddy only got worse, very weak, and very short of breath. On February 3, 1999, the doctors placed a pacemaker and defibulator in him to control his heart rate.

Momma got deathly sick from the chemo and radiation. It was so hard to watch her become so sick that she could not eat and she became so frail, we felt so helpless. Momma had a head full of thick beautiful hair and she lost it all, along with a lot of weight. She fought the cancer with everything she had. The side effects of the chemo and radiation were to say the least, horrible.

Daddy would sit in his chair, which was once surrounded by his newspaper and junk food, now surrounded by a breathing treatment machine and tons of medication bottles, and no radio playing a ballgame and no sports channel on TV. Momma's chair became surrounded by cups of Bluebell ice cream, Jello, Ensure, and her cup of water. She would mostly sit in her chair so tired that she could hardly hold her head up.

Chapter 7

Please No More Radiation

John 14:26-27
KJV

"But the Comforter,
which is the Holy Ghost,
whom the Father will send in my name,
he shall teach you all things,
and bring all things to your
remembrance, whatsoever I have
said unto you.
Peace I leave with you,
My Peace I give unto you,
not as the world giveth,
give I unto you.
Let not your heart be troubled,
neither let it be afraid."

The cancer being in Momma's neck and the radiation being directed there affected her swallowing, her hearing, and vision. At this point, she questioned:

"I became so sick I thought I was dying—and at this point I began to pray that God would let me die. What happened to all that faith? Where was that wonderful trust I had that was so strong in the beginning? Where was that will to survive? Where was God when I needed Him so desperately? To make matters worse, I could no longer read my Bible or my books, this was a very important part of my daily life. I went into a depression where I could not pray or even talk to God. I wasn't angry with God about the cancer, but I was confused as to why I couldn't read or pray or why I was taken out of church, why I had to give up my Sunday school class? Does God get angry when our faith wonders and we ask Him why? No, He doesn't? He completely understands, but there are some questions He may not decide to answer right away. So the best recourse is to trust God for an answer that will bring us to a place of peace in our hearts and minds. I finally asked God to give me an explanation to the best of my ability to understand and then I asked Him to restore my faith again. After many hours of talking to God I was given the answer—if I was going to die from the chemo treatment I would rather die from the cancer. At this time a wonderful peace came over my entire body. Yes, God gave me the answer.

She told Daddy and us children her decision and we all agreed with her. When she saw her Oncologist on her next visit she told her the decision she had made and the doctor agreed with her, no more chemo.

Although Daddy had the pacemaker placed, he struggled. For a man who was healthy as a horse, he was in and out of the hospital. He could not stand to be sick and lay in a hospital bed.

However, he would always put his hand along the side of our faces and smile and say, baby, the sun will come up again tomorrow. His quiet faith, his strong faith in God, his Father,

I believe with all of my heart never wavered. If it did, no one ever knew it.

Daddy knew with all that was in him, that joy would come in the morning. He held onto Psalms 30:5. He was not sure which morning and which sunrise, but it would come.

Chapter 8

Daddy Needs a Miracle and Momma struggles

1 John 4:7-12
KJV

"Beloved, let us love one another,
for love is of God; and everyone that
loveth is born of God and knoweth God.
He that loveth not knoweth not God;
for God is love.
In this was manifested the love of God
toward us, because that God sent his
only begotten Son in to the world, that
we might live through him.
Herein is love, not that we loved God,
but that He loved us, and sent his Son to
be the propitiation for our sins.
Beloved, if God so loved us, we ought
also to love one another."

April of 1999, Daddy became very sick. We took him to the hospital again. This time the doctors told us all that the only thing left was a new heart, a heart transplant. We stood there looking at that doctor as if to say *what did you just say?* Daddy hesitated, but said, "Okay." I believe that the only reason he say okay was for us: his beloved wife, children and grandchildren.

Momma's notebook reflects the exact date that Daddy was accepted: *Monday—April 19ᵗʰ found out he was approved to be on the list for a heart transplant.*

We were told he would be further down the list because he was still able to live at home and not as sick as others who where need of a heart transplant. We could only wait for a miracle; a touch from the Master's Hand, "the Great Physician." Faith is what we were standing on.

> **"A man's heart deviseth his way,**
> **But the Lord directeth his steps.**
> **The lot is cast into the lap,**
> **But the whole disposing thereof is of the Lord."**
> **Proverbs 16: 9, 33**
> **KJV**

But wait, a miracle for Daddy meant that another family would have to loose someone they loved. That was very hard for Daddy to accept, someone has to die for me to live. Daddy was torn over this concept, but he had to accept it. We didn't know anyone that had gotten a heart transplant. To have the heart that God made you with taken out, actually removed and someone else's heart would replace it. It was almost too much to comprehend.

Momma wrote her feelings: *"God laid it upon my heart that if I am not healed of this cancer that in the end my heart will be used for him, that he will be given a second chance to glorify God."*

These are words that she had never shared; it was overwhelming to me to read this, but that is love and that is the love she had for her precious husband. She wanted Daddy to have a second chance, not only to live, but to continue to glorify their God.

Momma continued to struggle with the long term affects of the cancer treatment. She lost her hearing in both ears and continued to have difficulty swallowing. She went through so many different hearing devices until she finally had the implanted one. This did help, but she had to carry the other part of it either in her pocket or safety pinned to her shirt. We had to make light of it. The grandchildren said Gammaw has an antenna on her head. She would role her big eyes at all of us, but I know she had to smile inside. When she would get in the car or was reaching for something in the refrigerator she would almost always bump the antenna. She fought with it buzzing when someone would get close to her.

She had chronic anemia, dizziness, and tired most of the time. She had numerous blood transfusions, which would help for a while. On the bright side, her beautiful hair grew back and was an awesome color of light brown and a soft white, she was beautiful.

Momma writes: *"Sometimes the only way some of us will submit ourselves to God's plan is to go through anguish, pressures, trials, and pain. Was this God's way of telling me something very important? I don't know the answer yet, but God now has my complete faith that He will show His plan when He is ready."*

Chapter 9

Daddy Gets a Miracle

Isaiah 40:31
KJV

"But they that wait upon the Lord
Shall renew their strength;
They shall mount up with wings
like eagles,
They shall run and not be weary;
They shall walk and not faint."

The winter of 1999, we were all at Momma and Daddy's house. It was Christmas. We all sat down to eat and Daddy blessed the food, as he always did. Momma and Daddy loved it when their family was together. I think all of us had gone to our own homes. A simple sentence is written by Momma; *December 26th at 10pm-Got "the call" to come to New Orleans for the new heart.* They have a heart for Daddy. It had only been 6 months, how did this happen so fast, it was a miracle, the miracle that we all prayed for. We all met in New Orleans at the Hospital. We had waited on God and kept our faith. I can't explain how we were all feeling. I don't think any of us knew how to feel. They told us the heart was coming in from up north somewhere and it was being transported by airplane.

It was very sad that we were told the donor family wanted to stay anonymous. We all wanted to say thank you and express feelings about their loss, but we had no choice but to accept their request. We could only pray that God would help them in this time of loss of their loved one, with knowing that their loss would allow Daddy to live. We just wanted to hug their neck and say I'm so sorry, but then again how can you say thank you in the same sentence. My aunt wrote a letter about Daddy to the donor's family and gave it to the social worker to give to them. At least they could know a little something about the one that received their loved one's heart.

They took Daddy back to the operating room until the heart got there. Another simple entry in the notebook: *December 27th Monday 7:30am new heart arrived at the hospital-began surgery-surgery completed 10:30am.*

I remember my sister and me sitting close to the elevators. It was very early the next morning, the elevator doors opened and a man pulling an ice chest got off. He was headed to the operating room. I looked at my sister and told her there goes Daddy's new heart. Sure enough, within a few minutes the nurse called and said they had started the surgery.

It was crazy, like something you would see on a movie. Momma didn't say a word. She mostly sat with her eyes closed, holding her water cup. She was praying, she was asking God to be in that room where her beloved husband lay. We all prayed, kind of easing to a quiet alone area in that waiting room.

We had no idea of what lay ahead of us now. Daddy was in ICU, then the transplant floor. A part of the transplant was steroids for anti-rejection. Daddy did not do well with high doses of steroids; he went in to a steroid induced psychosis. It was terrible. He was hallucinating. The doctors decided to put him in a drug induced coma. We said, "You want to do what?" So, they did and he was put on the ventilator. Momma was devastated, we all were. We found out the hard way that Daddy did not tolerate many medications and had to deal with the side-effects as they would occur and then they would change the medication. Thank God that Daddy did not know what was going on and didn't remember any of it. He was eventually weaned off the ventilator and things started looking up. Momma would sit at his bedside and read her books or write and then stare at Daddy, watching his every breath.

She was still fighting infections, mostly in her ears. I know that her strength only came from God. There is no one or nothing that can give you enough strength to see and go through everything we watched happen to Daddy except through God. His Holy Spirit guided us through every step of every day. After a few weeks, Daddy was transferred to an apartment, for transplant patients, by the hospital. He and Momma stayed there for a week or so. All of us kids would go and stay with them when we could. Momma had to get use to giving Daddy all of the new anti-rejection medications for the heart. They were able to come home in February.

They were both wore out and exhausted from everything, but they were home, their place of refuge and peace, no doctors and nurses everywhere, no getting stuck for blood, no more getting woken up when you finally got to sleep after hours of laying and looking at the ceiling tiles. The battle was fought and won. Daddy had a new heart! Home in the chairs of comfort. Again, they sat side by side. The next few months would be hurdles that would carefully be jumped over. Many trips back to New Orleans for follow up visits for Daddy and, for Momma, follow up visits in Jackson.

Chapter 10

Cancer Again

2 Corinthians 4:8-9
KJV

"We are troubled on every side,
yet not distressed;
we are perplexed;
but not in despair;
Persecuted,
but not forsaken;
cast down,
but not destroyed."

Momma continued to fight infections of the ears and would take rounds of antibiotics that seemed to never clear it up. She writes: *"September 18, 2000, had cat scan. The doctor called with the results, "There is something in there, about the size of a small marble, wants to do a biopsy on Friday 9/22/00. Monday 9/25/00 report of the biopsy—positive and surgery scheduled for Monday 10/2/2000."* It was the same type of cancer she had before. How could this be?

The surgeon had to do a radical neck surgery; this included removing a lot of the lymph nodes from the neck leaving Momma with large indentions in the neck. She hated this and how it made her look. She became embarrassed by her appearance. She would then wear shirts and scarves that would try and hide the scars and missing tissue.

Daddy was able to be there, but he wasn't feeling right. He was short of breath and couldn't walk very far. Momma was able to come home on the 4th.

On the 5th, my sister took Daddy to New Orleans for this breathing problem he was having. Tests were done and eventually it was found that there was a hole in the new heart. This even confused the doctors, how can this be, a hole in the new heart? We thought, *"No, not again. Lord, please help!"*

They could not do surgery because Daddy had a blood clot in his leg. So a surgery was done to put in a Greenfield filter to protect Daddy's heart from the clot.

Momma wrote: *"The surgeon came by and surgery is scheduled at 6am tomorrow, December 7th, could take 3-6 hours. He has not given me a good feeling about this surgery at all. He doesn't know how or why this hole came about; I am so worried and scared, much more than any surgery."*

They got Momma and Daddy's permission for video cameras to be in the operating room. The surgeon's hand and eyes were guided by God. He immediately found the hole, sewed it up, and saw what had happened. The new heart was tilted a little different than his heart that he was born with so the blood flow was going to the place where the new heart was attached. This constant blood flow had made the hole.

A note from Momma: *"Don't know how to explain it!! We have another Miracle!!! God lead the surgeon's hand straight to the problem, he fixed it in 35 minutes."*

The surgeon called Daddy the miracle man. I have to agree, our whole family would agree. We went back through the psychosis with the steroids again, not as bad as before. They were able to go home on December 12th.

I have to say right here, God never said the cross would not be heavy. He never promised us a rose garden in life. Although, *"He promised that when we walked through the valley of the shadow of death, He would be with us and that He would comfort us. He would lead us by the still waters."* Psalm 23. At this time we needed God's still waters, not the rapids of a rushing river. We had to be still and know that God was God. We had to put all of our trust in Him. Life seemed so uncertain, literally from day to day.

Momma loved the book of Job. As you read this book, I know that you see why bad things happened to Job again and again and again. He knew God was with him. Momma found faith in that and Daddy knew the sun would come up on a new tomorrow.

Chapter 11

Prayers Needed for Their Son

Psalm 69:1-3
KJV

"Save me, Oh God;
For the waters have come in unto my soul.
I sink in deep mire,
where there is no standing;
I am come in to deep waters,
where the floods overflow me.
I am weary of my crying;
my throat is dried;
Mine eyes fail while I wait for my God."

A few years had passed with continued illnesses for Momma and Daddy, but the illnesses were improving. In March of 2004, a different kind of pain showed up.

Momma's prayers at this time were within her and not written. They were not for her or for Daddy, this was different.

This time it was my older brother. We got a call from his wife. She had told us that my brother came home from work, called her, and told her that he wasn't feeling well. He wasn't sure what was going on. She immediately went home to check on him. She took him to the emergency room. She told us that he had had a heart attack. Our hearts sank, this could not be happening. Our first thought was to get on a plane and go there. His wife told us that a helicopter was taking him to a heart hospital in Montana and my brother said, "Don't come yet, he was okay." Momma and Daddy were in Mississippi and we were in Louisiana, we all prayed. Daddy never said, but with his history, we knew he was very concerned. We prayed and waited. My sister-in-law called back and the doctors had completed a heart catherization, found a blockage, and fixed the blockage. Praise God! He was weak, but he was okay. He would have to make some life style changes and was put on some medication.

It was a relief when we were able to hear his voice on the phone. It was a tough situation, we were all the way down south and they were up north and at that time all we wanted to do was see them. We knew there was distance for God; He was with everyone of us. They reassured us that they were okay and didn't want us to come up there and there was nothing really for us to do.

This was tough on Momma and Daddy, when dealing with their own illnesses it was different than dealing with an almost tragedy with one of their children.

Life can throw us a curve at any time and sometimes it can be back to back. Just when you think that we have made it through the valley and are up on the mountain and taking a sigh of relief, life continues on.

Chapter 12

Loosing Their First Born

Psalm 88:1-3
KJV

"O Lord God of my salvation,
I have cried day and night before thee:
Let my prayer come before thee:
incline thine ear unto my cry;
for my soul is full of troubles:
and my live draweth near the grave."

About 6 months after my older brother had a heart attack and recovered, life tragedy's continued. Why? This reminded me of Peter's faith when he stepped out of the boat and walked on the water toward Jesus, but as soon as he "saw the wind was boisterous, he was afraid and began to sink, he cried, saying, Lord save me." (Matthew 14:30 KJV) Where did his faith go? I guess like the wind, life shows up and our faith goes down.

How strong does your faith in God have to be when you get a phone call that a loved one has passed away? How does God help you through the most difficult loss of your life? How do parents get through the loss of a child?

Well, now that is what Momma and Daddy had to face. Their beloved first-born son had passed away. It was a very sudden heart attack. No warning, no nothing.

I don't know who said that a child should never go before the parents, but it's true. Even through the cancer and the heart, this was the ultimate pain. Again there are no written words in the notebook, but we all could see and feel the devastating pain and hurt in both of them.

He was the first born out of the love they had for each other. He was certainly very special; he carried the name of both Momma's Daddy and Daddy's Daddy.

This was a pain that surgery, medication, hospital, doctors, nothing could take away. This pain was unfixable, non-repairable, and cut to the very soul of Momma and Daddy.

Daddy had another hole in his heart, this one was inoperable and now Momma had a void in her heart. A physical part of them was gone and nothing could change it, nothing could bring back their precious son. They had loved him since he came into their world 50 years before. This loss affected them forever.

I can't write how their faith was at this point; they did not say. This was personal only between them and God. I can only imagine Daddy thinking, "My heart was bad, and did I pass this on to my sons." The words why, why my son and not me? He knew the family my brother left behind, why?

This was truly a time in their life that they had to draw close to God so they would not go absolutely crazy.

They had to trust in God more than all of the other times in their life. This happened in October 2004.

Chapter 13

Daddy falls and breaks His Hip

Romans 14:7-8
KJV

"For none of us liveth to himself,
and no one dieth to himself.
For whether we live, we live
unto the Lord;
and whether we die,
we die unto the Lord.
whether we live therefore, or die,
we are the Lord's."

In 2005, while at home, Daddy took a horrible fall. He was getting out of the bed at night and fell. He broke his hip. Momma called the ambulance because he could not move and she could not help him up. This put him back in the hospital, where he did not want to be.

I remember looking at him laying on that hard gurney in the emergency room and seeing the despair on his face. He was in pain because of the hip fracture and his back. He could not get comfortable, no matter what we tried to do to help him. I feel like that was the time that Daddy wanted to give up and say okay I have had enough. Of course, he would never say this out loud. He was strong for us, for Momma. However, the pain on his face and in his voice hurt more than any words he didn't say. We knew Momma could only sit there and hold her head in her hands. If I could read her mind, she too, was asking why? To be honest, I was too. How much more could my parents take?

"For My thoughts are not your thoughts,
neither are your ways my ways, saith the Lord.
For as the heavens are higher than the earth,
so are my ways higher than your ways,
and my thoughts than your thoughts."
(Isaiah 55:8-9 KJV)

We have to stay in the race. We can not do anything without our faith in God.

"But without faith it is impossible to please him: for he
that cometh to God must believe that he is, and that he is a
rewarder of them that diligently seek him."
(Hebrew 11:6)

Giving up is not an option, Daddy taught us that and now he has to set that example for us.

He had the hip replacement surgery. Now he was having more pain and becoming more dependent on Momma. He used a walker to get around. Our family doctor ordered a motorized wheelchair to help. Loosing more of his independence was harder for Daddy than the pain, although it all went together.

Momma watched him fight and struggle through it all. She was not a physically strong person, she's tiny and her little body was still so frail.

Chapter 14

Leaving Home

Psalm 90:10, 12, 14
KJV

"The days of our years
are threescore years and ten;
and if by reason of strength they be
fourscore years, yet is their strength
labour and sorrow;
For it is soon cut off, and we fly away."
(verse 10)
"So teach us to number our days, so that
we may gain our hearts unto wisdom."
(verse 12)
"O satisfy us early with
thy mercy; that we may rejoice
and be glad all our days."
(verse 14)

It was a very big decision, but Momma and Daddy decided to sell the home they had built together. It was a beautiful home. It set on about 5 acres. It was on the land that was given to Daddy by his parents. It was a place of his roots. Momma's beautiful flower beds that she worked so hard in, she could no longer keep up. Daddy could not cut the grass; the lawnmower was too hard for him to sit on. The house was too big for Momma to keep clean. It seemed everything was just too hard. He did not want to leave, but with rapidly declining health and a lot of prayer the decision was made.

So they sold the house and land and bought a mobile home in Louisiana, where we live. What a sacrifice. We were able to eventually move the mobile home onto our property. We could walk over any time and we were right beside them to help. Daddy was closer to his doctors, when he needed them. We tried so hard to make it *Home* for them. We built a deck for them to sit on in their rocking chairs. We had to build a ramp for Daddy to get the motorized wheelchair in and out. He used a walker when he wasn't too hard—headed to use it. Still with the chairs side by side they would sit.

They could no longer go to church and that was hard for them. My youngest daughter's preacher and his wife would visit them. Their preacher and his wife from Mississippi would come as often as they could to visit with them. The Hope Sunday school class came one day and they all went out to eat. Daddy was embarrassed to use the walker or the wheelchair, most of the time he would grin and bear it, best he could.

His eyes were so bad from cataracts he could hardly see. The television was kept on CNN with an occasional ballgame. My brother and parents would joke, "Momma can't hear the TV and Daddy can't see it so they have to let each other know what was going on." We would all laugh; that's what we had to do sometimes to get through everything. That was Daddy's nature to laugh or make jokes at the hard stuff. When he would get out of his chair he would sometimes muster up the energy to dance a little jig. Other times he would holler with pain getting up to walk. Momma did all she could do and most of all make sure he had his breakfast, lunch and supper and always baking cookies and her famous fudge for his snack. She stayed so weak herself, but that was her life to take care of Daddy.

Chapter 15

Daddy's Transplant heart had a Heart Attack

Psalm 23:4, 6
KJV

"Yea, though I walk through
the valley of the shadow of death,
I will fear no evil:
for thou art with me;
thy rod and thy staff,
they comfort me." (verse 4)
"Surely goodness and mercy
shall follow me
all the days of my life:
and I will dwell
in the house of the Lord
forever." (verse 6)

When Daddy got the heart transplant the doctors said it was good for about 7 years. He surpassed that, by the Glory of God, but almost exactly 10 years later the new heart had a heart attack, January 2009. We were back in the hospital. It was at that time Daddy said, "That's enough." He put his life in God's hands. The doctors wanted to do a procedure that may or may not help. Daddy said, "I'm going home". Momma cried. She said, "I can not live without him!"

My sister and I were there when the nurse came in. This is the nurse who had been with Daddy when he had the transplant; she knew everything that he had been through. She told him, "It's okay, it's your choice." I guess Daddy needed to hear that from her, although he had already made his decision. She was an angel sent by God. She knew that Daddy had placed himself in God's hands. She even talked about his faith.

I told Daddy, "You got the heart for us, now it's time for you to do what you want to do." Daddy looked at my sister and told her, "Just make sure you get my body back to Mississippi when I die." She ran out in the hallway and cried.

The doctor discharged Daddy that day. He talked about hospice care and Daddy did not want any part of that; although, he did agree to home health care.

Home health became a part of our life. God sent another angel, his home health nurse. She was "tiger girl" from LSU, that's what Daddy called her. His teasing her became fun for him. She never knew what to expect from Daddy when she walked in the door. Since Daddy was Ole Miss all the way, the game was on.

Over the next year, Daddy lived on pain medication to get through the back pain. The doctors did as much as they could do. Momma got back into her oil paintings and sewing. This was her saving grace. Life was a challenge on a daily basis. Daddy wanted to know, what would happen if he stopped taking some of the anti-rejections medications for the heart? I called the transplant nurse. She said that he would probably slowly die. It was Daddy's choice and at that time he decided to get off one of the medications.

One day, while Daddy was taking a nap, momma asked me, "What do I do? I can not live without him." I didn't know the answer, but all I knew was that we would have to take one day at a time.

She wanted them to go together, but how? She always dream of it being like a movie that she had seen, where a married couple just laid down, went to sleep and passed away holding each other. I still had no answer for her except that I would be there for her and Daddy, and we would make it together. I didn't know it at the time, but she had planted a faith seed that day.

During all of this, another why was occurring in our lives? My sister-in-law was diagnosed with breast cancer a month before all of that happened with Daddy. While we were all in the hospital with Daddy, she was having a mastectomy. We were all devastated, especially Momma. She was so upset that her daughter-in-law may have to go through chemotherapy and radiation. Momma knew the illness that went with that kind of treatment and she prayed for her daughter-in-law. Her soul cried to God, "No, no, please God spare her from this."

We all praised God when we got the call that the doctor had told her she would not need the treatment. God had answered Momma's prayers, all of our prayers. We were so thankful!

The scripture says, **"Blessed be God, even the Father of our Lord Jesus Christ, the Father of mercies and the God of all comfort; who comforteth us in all our tribulation, that we may be able to comfort them which are in any trouble, wherewith we ourselves are comforted by God."**
(2 Corinthians 1:3-4 KJV)

Chapter 16

Why Cancer Again?

Hebrews 4:16
KJV

"Let us therefore come boldly
unto the throne of grace,
that we might obtain
mercy, and find grace
to help in time
of need."

Momma would have to go to the doctor to get her throat stretched because of the long term effects of the radiation and the surgery to her neck. She had atrophy of the muscles to the left shoulder and usually would wear a brace to hold the shoulder up. The swallowing was always a problem and the hearing difficulties drove her crazy sometimes.

Momma's anemia was an ongoing battle. She was having dizzy spells and falling. She went to the doctor. January of 2010, the doctors scheduled her for a colonoscopy they thought she may be loosing blood that way and that would be what was causing the anemia. We left home that morning to have the test. My husband and mother-in-law stayed with Daddy.

They called me back to recovery after the test. The doctor came to Momma and me and told us that she had cancer in her colon. He said that she would need surgery to remove it.

She began to weep uncontrollably. She said, "No I have to take care of your Daddy." She was almost angry! I took her hand and made her look at me. I said, "Let's pray." I prayed that God was in control of this situation; He would give us the strength we needed to get through this; he would remove the cancer and everything would be fine.

I think now that I would never know how much God was in control; His foreseeable knowledge had a plan.

At that time, I was on a 21 day fast with my church. This was my first fast, and with this fast I remembered that the bible states, "THIS only comes through prayer and fasting." (Matthew 17:21) Well, I had no idea what the THIS for me was going to be, but I am positively sure that if I had not been at that place in my life, then I don't know how I would have handled the days to follow. God is an awesome God; His Bible is true, and the words in it are to be used in life and not just read. What my parents had taught me about God and faith were drawn out of me at that time, stronger than ever. For me to be the youngest, I always had to be the strongest. Daddy expected that from me, he never told me why.

As we prayed there in that recovery room, Momma's faith began to rise up in her and a Peace came over her. She stopped crying and began to give me orders. She said, "Call your sister and tell her we need her, we need her to take care of Daddy and you will be with me." That's exactly what I did. Trying to keep it together I called my sister and she said, "I'm on my way."

Momma and I went home and told Daddy about the cancer; his eyes began to tear. Momma sat on the floor in front of him and laid her head in his lap. We left them to be alone.

Momma wrote this several years before the 3rd cancer was diagnosed.

"Each of us have had or will have adversities come into our lives. I know my cancer will not be my last. But when they do come our way, we are able to learn from our past experiences of pain and how much we grow spiritually and to let God lead us through and determine how we live through the future pain, trials, and tribulations.

Yes, God has a plan for our lives, a Master plan. God's love is greater for each of us than we could ever imagine. His ultimate goal is to bring us to a maturity in Christ Jesus. I may not see any purpose for some of the troubles that come my way, but God always has a purpose in everything.

My first response when adversity comes into my life is to turn to God and ask, "God tell me what is going on." He will continue to be with you and me in the future.

Our lives have a purpose far beyond comfort, ease, or pleasure. Our lives are intended to be used by God to fulfill His purposes on this earth. To God Be the Glory-Amen."

Chapter 17

Momma had Surgery

John 14: 16-17
KJV

"And I will pray the Father,
and he shall give you another Comforter,
that He may abide with you forever;
Even the Spirit of truth;
whom the world cannot receive,
because it seeth him not:
neither knoweth him:
but ye know him,
for He dwelleth with you
and shall be with you."

We tried to celebrate Momma's birthday on January 14th. We brought her a spring bouquet of flowers, and she got gifts from the kids. She was now the oldest for the year. She was now 76 years old.

Her surgery was scheduled on January 20th. This was on a Wednesday. My sister stayed at home with Daddy and I helped Momma get in my truck. She began crying. I looked over at her and said, "What is it, Momma?" She told me, "I don't want to leave him." These words became very real over the next few days. She stopped crying and said, "Let's go." So we did.

Her spirits lifted and as we waited for the surgery in the pre-operative area. She was visited by their home church pastor and his wife from Mississippi. She let him pray for her and then told them to go and stay with Daddy and they did. We prayed another prayer before she went back that God would remove all of the cancer. I need to say that I learned from that prayer sometimes maybe I need to be more specific. The surgeon came out after surgery and all of the cancer was removed.

However, Momma began to have complications. The doctor told us that she had had a heart attack in recovery. I exclaimed, "What! Daddy was the one with all the heart problems, now Momma?" God did what I asked in my prayer, and the cancer was removed. But now she has had a heart attack.

They took Momma to ICU. It seemed like forever before they let us go back and see her. When we did, she was awake and talking, kind of in and out, but better than I expected. My sister brought Daddy to see her the next day, such sadness on his face. They held hands and had spoke very few words.

Things seemed to be getting better. She was waking up and talking and we all thought she was going to be okay. We thought she would be going to a room on one of the units and getting out of ICU.

The following Sunday, my sister had gone to visit Momma and my husband stayed with Daddy, I went to church. Remember I'm still fasting. A friend came up to me in the worship service and told me that *God told her to tell me that He would give me strength to get through this day.* It didn't hit me until later what she meant. When I got in my truck after the service I saw on my phone where my sister had called. I called her back and she said get to the hospital Momma is worse; she was going to be with Daddy. When I got to the hospital the nurses let me go back to the ICU even though visiting hours were over. I walked in and all the nurses were in there I asked what is going on. I was told that she was retaining fluid in her lungs, she had pneumonia. I have to say at this point, I am a register nurse, I looked at Momma's catheter bag and it was full, she was not swollen. I could not speak. Don't ask me why, because usually I'm all over the situation. God shut my mouth; He was in control. I was told that she refused to be put on a ventilator that morning. I knew that she and Daddy had already had that discussion. They were going to put an oxygen mask on her. Morphine had been given to her to calm her down; it's hard not to become anxious when you can't breath.

Chapter 18

Momma First?

John 14:1-4
KJV

"Let not your heart be troubled,
ye believe in God,
believe also in Me.
In My Father's house are many
mansions; if it were not so,
I would have told you,
I go to prepare a place for you.
And if I go to prepare a place for you.
I will come again,
and receive you unto myself;
that where I am ye may be also.
And whither I go ye know,
and the way ye know."

She opened her eyes and looked at me; as if to say its okay God is in control.

I was told to call the family. I called my sister and Daddy and told them to get come now. I called my brother and his wife, my husband, my oldest daughter, and when I called my youngest daughter and her husband she began to call everyone else.

My sister brought Daddy there, he held Momma's hand. She opened her eyes a little to look at him. His heart was again broken. Tears began to swell up in his eyes. He knew it was time. He and Momma had talked before about any life support, and he knew her wishes. He told them to take off the oxygen mask. That was the hardest words that Daddy ever had to say, but he was the only one who could say it. He said, "I have to go" as he was frantically trying to move the wheelchair he was in out of the tiny ICU room. He could not sit there and watch his precious wife die, he just couldn't. My sister took him home. The mask that covered all of Momma's tiny face was removed. I just stood there; I didn't know what to do. By then, my husband, youngest daughter, her husband, and their daughter were at the hospital.

All I could do was crawl in the bed and hold my Momma. The room seemed so quiet. I could feel God's presence. He was there. I laid there holding Momma as my family kept coming in and out of the room or looking through the glass window, they did not know what to do. I laid there holding her as I listened to the heart monitor, as it began to slow down and mine speeding up, and then her heart stopped. There was no more beating of her heart. I laid there holding her crying, *"No! No! Momma!"* I finally became silent and just held her and told her how much I loved her.

The nurses came in, but they gave me my time and I thanked them for that. My daughter came in the room I looked at her and told her, *"I don't know what to do."* She told me, "Her spirit is gone; we have to let her go." She was trying so hard to be strong for me. She got me out of Momma's bed and held me in her arms, we cried together. I asked the doctor, "Did we do the right thing?" and she said, "Yes" I had to know that. I got her clothes and personal things together. My family had to just about carry me to the truck. I went straight to Daddy and held him whispering in his ear, "She's gone." He could not speak, and he just held me. There were no other words to say. Our hearts were again broken, we lost Momma.

It was an awful but yet beautiful experience. I thought, *"Momma held me when I came in the world and I held her as she left this world, I would not have had it any other way."* I knew Momma went to be with God. There was a peace in that ICU room as strange as that sounds. I felt God's Presence in that room. He was there. "He was not going to leave me or forsake me." (Hebrew 13:5)

But now, what about Daddy?

Chapter 19

Momma's Funeral

John 10:27-29
KJV

"My sheep hear my voice,
and I know them, and they follow me:
And I give unto them eternal life;
and they shall never perish,
neither shall any man pluck them out of
my hand. My Father, which gave them
me, is greater than all;
and no man is able to pluck them out of
My Father's hand."

Momma passed on Sunday January 24, 2010; it was about 6:30pm. I can just see Momma walking the streets of gold, gazing at all the beautiful colors. She probably stood there in awe. Now she could really have church in the garden of heaven with God and all the others who went before her. I know that people say, "When I get to heaven I have so many questions for God." I believe when we get to heaven our memories are wiped clean of all the questions we asked back here on earth. It's not a time of questions. It's a time of praise and worship to our Creator, Redeemer, and Almighty God.

I thought, *"My Lord, what can we do for him?"* His love, high school sweetheart, mother of his children, and wife of 58 years was no longer sitting beside him. He was lost! *"Dear Lord, please help him."*

We all got loaded up and headed home to Mississippi. We were able to stay with our sweet aunt. She was very close to my parents. We carried all Daddy's medication for the week, oxygen tank, his walker, and wheelchair. He was so weak. Daddy, my sister, and her oldest daughter, and I went to pick out the casket. There were so many caskets in that cold room, but we knew Momma wanted something simple. We all agreed on a beautiful wooden one with off-white satin on the inside. Then we had to pick out the headstone. We looked through a book of them, finally finding one that was a lot like Daddy's parents. We ordered a double head stone. I called my brother and described the headstone and casket to him, Daddy wanted him to have a say in our choices.

I remember Momma told me not to leave the casket open. She said, "I don't want every body staring at me." I smiled at her and said, "I will leave the casket open and you want be here to fuss at me when I do." Boy, did I get those big green eyes thrown at me. She laughed because she knew I was right and there was nothing she could do about it. My sister and I were the ones to put a little make up on Momma and to do her hair. She looked beautiful, peaceful, no worries, and no cares. We got everything set up with the preacher. He loved Momma and Daddy so much.

My brother was so upset because where he lived, up north, he was snowed in. He might have been able to drive to the airport, but it was several hours away, but it was dangerous. So he had to write a letter about Momma for me to read. We had her service at the chapel of the funeral home so it would be easier on Daddy. He did good talking to all of the people that came to the funeral home. He attempted smiles and shook hands. Of course, many memories were shared. A lot of their high school classmates came. That made Daddy very happy because he had not seen them all in a long time. Although the smiles he had were only for the moment. He tried to comfort all of the grandchildren, seven in all, and nine great-grandchildren. Their preacher had wonderful words to say. He recalled the first time he met Momma and how she kind of sat and checked him out as he talked to Daddy. He had to pass her test, so to speak, and he recalls that he passed the test.

We had the graveside service at the church. My wonderful Pastor and his wife drove up from Louisiana. He prayed at the grave.

The songs that were chosen were beautiful, such as, "In the Garden". I'm sure Momma's garden on earth could not compare to the gardens in Heaven. I can see her looking at the beauty of heavenly flowers and the majestic colors. "I'll sure miss you" was another song because in our minds Heaven was sweeter with her there.

Chapter 20

Then God Called Daddy

"Oh death where is your sting?
O Hades, where is your victory?
The sting of death is sin,
and the strength of sin is the law.
But thanks be to God,
who gives us the victory through
Christ Jesus."

(1 Corinthians 15: 55-57, KJV)

We brought Daddy back to Louisiana, on a Thursday, after the funeral. He was exhausted. He could hardly climb up the steps. He just wanted to get in his bed. For the man who loved to talk and laugh, now life was silent with very few words and very few smiles. We got him in his bed.

At this point, my sister had moved in with him. Together we would take care of him. Over the next few days, I took over giving him his medication, filling the weekly pill planner. Daddy's appetite was gone. He could only take a few bites of something and then just lie back in his chair and close his eyes.

He knew that my sister and I would take care of him, but God knows it was not the same as Momma.

On Saturday, ten days after we left Momma in Mississippi. It was a quiet day; Daddy told me several times to make sure I sent the thank you cards for all of the flowers that were sent for Momma. I sat at the wooden kitchen table and did what he said.

About 6:00 pm I had walked to my house. A few minutes later, my sister called me and said Daddy is breathing strange. I ran back over there. We started his breathing treatment to see if that would help. It did some, or at least he said it did. I kneeled down on the floor and looked him straight in the face and asked him, "What do you want me to do?" He just looked at me, as if to say you already know. Yes, I did know. He had already told me, "Do not take me back to the hospital." However, the words came out of my mouth anyway. He looked at me and said okay. I knew with all that was in me that he did not mean it. We looked into each others eyes, his little sweet blue eyes, and I knew. It was like he was saying to me it's time baby girl, but he didn't have to say anything, he was ready. He was ready to go to Heaven and see the God that he served and meet Jesus who was his Savior, and of course he wanted to see Momma.

We helped him into their bed, kissed him, and told him it would be alright. We told him we loved him and he said softly, "I love you too" as he placed his frail hand on the side of our faces. He closed his eyes. I called his home health nurse and told her it was time. We got hospice to come out. Daddy had refused hospice the day before. We called our family having no idea what to tell them and how long it would be. My brother and his wife were up north and the rest of the family was in Mississippi except for my girls and their families

At this time, the devastating sound of the death rattle was coming out of his mouth. It was happening. Daddy was dying right in front of my eyes.

My oldest daughter tried to come in the house, but she could hear his breathing from the door. She began to cry. I told her it's okay she didn't have to come in. I know it was hard for her to walk away, but it was harder for her to stay. Our youngest daughter, her husband, who loved Papa like he was his own, and their daughter came and stayed. When my son-in-law began to talk to Daddy he opened his eyes and tried to get up but he couldn't. My husband was there, but had no idea what to do. My step-son and his wife came as well.

My precious husband had no idea what to do so he called our Pastor. I don't know how, but he said as soon as he got off the phone with Pastor he saw headlights pull into the driveway. It was Pastor and his wife. My husband feels like it was the Hand of God that seemed to have already put them fully dressed and on their way to our house. It seemed as though Pastor was told by God something's going on, be ready.

By then the home health nurse, Tiger Girl, and the hospice nurse were there. We were in Daddy's room when Pastor and his wife came in. He called Daddy's name and Daddy sat up in the bed. My mouth dropped open. He could hear Pastor and he tried to turn to look at him. I think Pastor said I want to pray with you. Daddy said, "Okay." I can not remember the words, but Daddy laid back down.

The Holy Spirit in Daddy acknowledged the Holy Spirit in Pastor. It was a spiritual event that just happened. I can't explain any more than that.

The rattle returned and his eyes were closed again. Daddy's nurse sat on the floor by the bed and asked if there was anything else she could do. He told her, "No Tiger Girl, I think that's all."

It was getting late and everyone had left except my sister and I. My husband laid down in the bed in the back. My sister got in the bed and laid beside Daddy. I pulled up a chair at the foot of the bed. I counted every breath he took. I got Momma's bible out and read Psalm 91. I went and sat on the floor and took Daddy's hand and put it on the side of my face and I told him, "It's okay Daddy, you can go now." He didn't respond. My heart was broken, but there was a Peace in that room, a Peace that can only come from God. It was like the Peace that I had felt two weeks before as I laid holding Momma in that ICU room. I asked God, "Please don't let him suffer anymore." I closed my eyes as it was if I could feel angel's wings brushing on my face. Then as I prayed a time flashed through the mind . . . 3:30 am. My eyes popped open and I put the clock where I could see it.

All I could do was watch his chest rise up and down and hear every breath. I continued to watch the clock. It was somewhere around 3:15 am and I got up and sat on the floor beside him with his silver watch in my hand. Over the next 15 minutes his respirations got slower and slower. As I sat there, he took his last breath. All I could do is sit there and look at him. I took his hand and put it on my cheek and told him, *"I love you my Daddy."* His spirit was gone. His pain and suffering was gone.

Paul wrote in 2 Timothy; "I have fought the good fight, I have finished the race, I have kept the faith." That scripture was Daddy, he fought a hard and long fight, he finally finished the race, and most of all he kept his Faith. I am proud to say that's Daddy.

I reached over Daddy and told my sister he's gone. She held him in her arms and wept.

I called the hospice nurse, told my husband, and called everyone, I guess I called everyone. The hospice nurse came back. Hospice was good to have; she called the funeral home and made arrangements. It wasn't too long after she called the funeral home that the precious lady that helped us with Momma two weeks before called, she could not believe it.

My son-in-law came back as soon as I called. He held me in his strong arms and I cried like a child. I could always do that with him. Bless his heart he held my sister, too. He also helped them carry daddy out of the house. Oh, he loved him so very much.

Daddy passed on February 7, which was 2 weeks from the day Momma had passed.

Chapter 21

Daddy's Funeral

2 Timothy 4:7-8
KJV

"I have fought a good fight,
I have finished my course,
I have kept the faith:
Henceforth there is laid up for me
a crown of righteousness, which the
Lord, the righteous judge,
shall give me on that day:
and not only me,
but unto all them also that love his
appearing."

We got Daddy back to Mississippi just like we promised. The same type of casket was chosen, so we did not have to go back into that room. The headstone was already ordered, we just had to add Daddy's name to it. We again called our brother and told him what we had chosen. Daddy wanted him to be a part of Momma's so we knew he would want his son to be in on the choices for him as well. The same arrangement of flowers were put on the casket.

Everything seemed to just fall into place. The only thing that was done different is that Daddy's service was at the church, his church. The service was not until Friday, my brother and his wife were able to get out of the snowy weather this time. The funeral home was once again full of family and friends. Everyone saying I can't believe this, *"Just two weeks."*

The evening before the service, it snowed. That Friday morning snow was all over the hills of southern Mississippi. The lady at the funeral home said that the National Guard would not be able to come from Jackson to play taps. At the funeral home was a young man in his army uniform, he was a friend of one of my nieces. We asked him if he would fold the American flag and he seemed honored to do so.

A lot of Daddy's friends and some family could not get back to the funeral home due to the icy roads. We were told that the grave diggers may not be able to get there. We got prepared. We had asked some people for shovels and help if we needed it, but the grave diggers were able to do it. The county made sure all of the bridges from the funeral home to the church were sanded over and cars could go over them safely. Daddy's preacher stayed at the church to wait on us.

We were all in the room where Daddy laid; there was no preacher to say a word of prayer for my Daddy. It was like Daddy whispered in my ear *you can do this.* My family all around, I stood by Daddy with my hand on his, and I prayed. God gave me the words because I'm not even sure what all I prayed. It was completely silent as we stood there, I took a deep breath. This is what I do remember . . . . *"Father, we thank you that you have taken Momma and Daddy together, neither left here without the other. I thank you Father God for the lives that they lived. Everyone in this room has a part of Daddy in them and Lord may we live the lives that would make him proud, and may we take a piece of his faith out of this room with us. We love you Father God and we thank you and Praise you."* I think I prayed more than that I just don't remember. The words came from my Father God, that's all I can say. As I walked out of that room, my Pastor and his wife were walking in the door. I was so happy to see them, but I knew God had wanted me to be the one that said the prayer.

We all lined up our cars behind the police car with their blue lights on. We carefully and cautiously drove out to the church. As we drove we saw white piles of snow on the sides of the road and snow in all the trees. It didn't snow very often there, but it was beautiful.

The songs were the ones Daddy loved; of course, "How Great Thou Art" was one. Daddy's friend and preacher preached a wonderful message. He told stories of Daddy, sweet memories. The young man in the army uniform very carefully folded the American flag that draped over the casket and handed it to my older bother. We wanted to play a song at the graveside, but it was too cold so we played it in the church, "Go Rest High on That Mountain," Daddy had told me once before he liked that song, and I remembered that.

The snow had stopped, but the whole cemetery was covered in white except where the grave diggers dug right next to Momma. It was that red Mississippi dirt. The dirt over her grave still freshly covered. The dirt Momma planted and prayed in. We walked out there with the snow crunching under our feet with every step.

Our Pastor spoke and he told of the night Daddy passed and how when he got there God's spirit moved in Daddy and he sat up for just a few seconds. I pictured that in my mind.

I can now see Momma and Daddy in Heaven together. I can imagine Momma waiting at the gate. Now together again, the way it should be, just like it had been for over 58 years on this earth, but now for eternity.

Daddy's old saying that the sun will come up tomorrow was over. God shall now be his everlasting light. He would no longer have to wait on the sun to rise in Heaven for God's glory is all the light he would desire in eternity.

Chapter 22

Heavenly Reunion

1 Corinthians 10:13
KJV

"There hath no temptation taken you, but
as is common to man;
but God is faithful,
who will not suffer you to be tempted
above that ye are able;
but will with the temptation
above that ye are;
but will with the temptation
also make a way to eascape, that ye
may be able to bear it."

God honors faith. His Word is true and He will not let us go through anything that He knows we are no able to bear. This is one of God's promises to us. It's a promise of a Heavenly Father who loves His children and will never let us down.

I believe with all that I am that Momma and Daddy sat down together and had a talk with God. Momma said so many times that she can not live without Daddy, and I know that Daddy felt the same. Maybe they talked to Him about His promise. The Bible says that His Word will not return to Him void. God is Faithful and knows the desires of all hearts. The Scripture could have also reminded them of Psalm 9:10 KJV. **"And they that know thy name will put their trust in thee; for thou, Lord, hast not forsaken them that seek thee."**

I believe that they came into an agreement with God before Momma went to the hospital to have the surgery and they all put that plan to work.

One thing I haven't mentioned is that when my sister and I were helping Daddy to his bed on the night he passed, was this . . . as we helped him through the kitchen to their bedroom, the smell of cookies filled the house. My sister and I both smelled the sweet aroma. It was so strong we looked at each other and said, *"Oh my."* It was like Momma was calling to him and saying; "Come on, we are waiting on you."

Now looking back I can almost see Momma and my oldest brother standing at the gate of Heaven in exciting anticipation of Daddy. Everyone in Heaven was waiting. She could hear now, she could hear the continual heavenly worship of God on His throne. Revelation 4:3 (KJV) states "and there was a rainbow round the throne in sight like unto an emerald." They could hear an ever present melody echoing with praise of "Holy, Holy, Holy, Lord God Almighty, who was and is to come." (Revelation 4:8).

The same welcoming committee that met Momma two weeks before was there for Daddy. A great family reunion took place. Not just an earthly family but a heavenly family as well. I pray that the young man who passed away and gave his heart to Daddy was standing there. Daddy could finally say thank you to him.

I can picture in my mind as that last breath he took was over, he stood in God's glory. He would be able stand tall without pain; he would join the hymns of praise maybe even that sweet voice would sing "How Great Thou Art."

In my mind, I can see them walking the streets of gold hand in hand.

Chapter 23

Peace in the Cemetery

Exodus 33:14
KJV

"And he said,
My Presence
shall go with thee,
and
I will give thee rest."

A year has passed and I sit at the cemetery in front of the head stones that bear Momma and Daddy's name. I praised God for His awesome Grace and wonderful Mercy. He loves us all so much; this is showed to us through the death, burial, and resurrection of His Son, Jesus Christ. I thanked Him for how He loved my parents and how He answered their prayer. God knows how hard it was for us to go through that, but God carried us through. He has given me a peace that passes all my human understanding.

As I sat there, I closed my eyes and it was if I could see Momma standing there with a smile. She couldn't get too close; it was though there was a void between us. She told me, "It's beautiful here" and Daddy came up behind her and told me, "It's so peaceful." His appearance was that of peace. I longed to know from each of them, *did I do everything right?* Did I follow through on everything exactly how they wanted me too? As always I sought approval from my parents.

As I sat there a beautiful peace blew across the graves. It seemed as if it was my answer. Inside I felt them say, "Yes baby girl you did, you did good."

I opened my eyes and looked around. I was in tears, tears of joy, not pain.

I say this not boasting, but it was the first of the year and our church was fasting again for 21 days. As I learned before, THIS can only happen through prayer and fasting. The THIS for me was a Spiritual meeting in the cemetery. I didn't want to leave.

I was given some wonderful words from my Pastor's wife when I told her to *please say a prayer for me it's coming up on a year of my parent's death*. She told me, "Try and look at it not as a year that they have been gone but try and celebrate a year of their being in Heaven." Wow, those were some wonderful words of encouragement.

Revelation 7:13-17 (KJV) states a wonderful image of what Heaven is:

And one of the elders answered, saying unto me, What are these which are arrayed in white robes? And whence came they? And

I said unto him, Sir, thou knowest. And he said to me, These are they that came out of great tribulation, and have washed their robes, and made them white in the blood of the Lamb. Therefore are they before the throne of God, and serve him day and night in his temple: and he that sitteth on the throne shall dwell among them. They shall hunger no more, neither thirst any more, neither shall the sun light on them, nor any heat. For the Lamb which is in the midst of the throne shall feed them, and shall lead them unto the living fountains of waters: and God shall wipe away all tears from their eyes.

Chapter 24

We Miss Them So Much

Revelation 21:4
KJV

"And God shall wipe away
all tears from their eyes;
there shall be no more death,
neither sorrow,
nor crying.
Neither shall there be any more pain,
for the former things are
passed away."

Even though, I am fully aware that God answered Momma and Daddy's prayer to go to Heaven together, to stand at the foot of the throne, and Praise God. I do not ask why, because I know what God did. It was by His love and mercy that He would not leave one here without the other.

I still have days that all I want to do is cry because I miss them so much. During certain times when something happens, the first thought is to pick up the phone and call them and share what ever is going on. As Daddy would say, *"just to hear their voices."* My heart is broken when I realize I can't do that.

I have learned that I miss them physically in my life. I miss their smiling faces, I miss Daddy's hand on my cheek, and I miss holding my little Momma. I want to hear Daddy's words of wisdom, sometimes I need to hear his advice. I miss that.

God, my Father, helped me through it all. He continues to be my strength, but sometimes I have to ask Him for His help.

I also get help from calling my brother and sister. My brother is so much like Daddy. I hear his voice on the phone and I hear some of Daddy. I call him now for advice. I look at my sister and she rolls her eyes at me and gives that Momma look.

Being there watching both of my parents take their last breath was so hard. It was so final. I think about it a lot. I can close my eyes and relive both events. God does give me strength.

I have to remember my experience at the cemetery where God gave me such peace. God gave me a gift that day, a gift that no one can take from me, a gift of His love and the love of my Momma and Daddy that will carry me through the rest of my life

They are missed so much by the grandchildren and the great-grandchildren. I let the children talk about them; I don't want them to forget. My oldest granddaughter and I were watching television one day and a commercial came on. It was a cute little doll. She said, "Gammaw can make that." She looked at me with big tears in my eyes; she ran and got in my lap. I told her, "It's okay, I want you to remember how her Gammaw would make Raggedy Ann and Andy dolls. It's happy memories!" We both cried, and I told her these are happy tears.

We have all the beautiful paintings that were done so carefully with Momma's little hands. Also Daddy's arrow head collections and . . . . of course . . . . I have the Notebook.